H.
L2123
5/7/74

60p

8JKY14

KU-102-388

Teaching a Child to Read

LIVERPOOL INSTITUTE OF
NOTRE DAME COLLEGE OF EDUCATION
HIGHER   EDUCATION MOUNT PLEASANT
THE BECK LIBRARY LIVERPOOL L3 5SP

# Teaching a Child to Read

W. E. C. Gillham

University of London Press Ltd

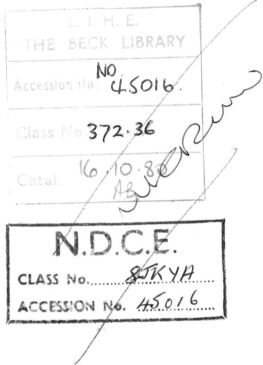

L. I. H. E.
THE BECK LIBRARY

Accession No. NO. 45016.

Class No. 372.36

Catal. 16/10.8

N.D.C.E.

CLASS No. 8JKYH

ACCESSION No. 45016

ISBN 0 340 16150 7   Boards
ISBN 0 340 17164 2   Paper

Copyright © 1974 W. E. C. Gillham

All rights reserved. No part of this publication may be reproduced or transmitted in any form or by any means, electronic or mechanical, including photocopy, recording, or any information storage or retrieval system, without permission in writing from the publisher.

University of London Press Ltd,
St Paul's House, Warwick Lane, London EC4P 4AH

Printed in Great Britain by
T. and A. Constable Ltd, Edinburgh

# Acknowledgments

My thanks are due to Gail Panasiuk who typed and re-typed the contents of this book; my wife who checked the grammar, punctuation and style; and my colleagues Angela White and Kenneth Hesse who made valuable constructive criticisms of the penultimate manuscript.

# Prefatory Note

## This book is intended for parents or others teaching an individual child to read

This is no 'miracle method'—there is none in learning to read—and it requires systematic work on the part of whoever undertakes the teaching. The whole book must be read through before any teaching begins, and each session must be carefully prepared.

The complete instruction programme is designed for children aged seven to eleven years who have not begun to read at all, or who can recognise only a few words. Children who can recognise quite a number of words by sight, but seem to be unable to make further progress, need instruction in phonics (the detailed learning of the sounds made by letters and combinations of letters); these children can start with Section Two (page 40).

The approach suggested is suitable for most children who are slow in learning to read, including the majority of that group, sometimes known as 'dyslexic', where the difficulty is relatively specific.

The design of the programme assumes that the child is using the traditional alphabet at school. It is not suitable for children whose schools use the Initial Teaching Alphabet (i.t.a.).

The entire programme takes about eighteen months to complete.

# Introduction

I have written this book because I felt that I could offer positive and practical help to many parents who were justifiably concerned about their children's reading standards. But let me insert a note of caution. If you have bought this book, or are thinking of buying it, you may have tried to help your child to read already. *If this well-meant attempt led to loss of temper, tears, tenseness, or general unpleasantness, then you are probably not the person to teach your child even with the most suitable programme. If you should force the matter, you will do your son or your daughter no good and you may well find that it has a detrimental effect on your relationship.* If this advice makes you feel rather despairing, as an alternative I suggest you might enlist the aid of a family friend or engage a remedial teacher who could use the methods I propose. Even then a similar caution applies: if it's a pleasant learning relationship, it will work; if it's not, it won't.

Before I go on to outline the ideas that lie behind this book, I think I should give some indication of my qualifications to write it. By this I do not mean formal qualifications; in themselves they mean very little. Briefly, I have studied psychology and education as academic subjects and have trained as both a teacher and a psychologist. I have also taught in primary and secondary schools. I think I was quite good at teaching reading, and I have become progressively better at understanding why children fail to learn to read. This is largely due to my experience of the past few years as an educational psychologist with two local education authorities. In this capacity I have seen, individually, many hundreds of children who have failed to read, and

I have talked to their teachers and their parents. This 'clinical' experience, by which I mean the detailed study of individual cases, is something which you do not have as a regular part of a teaching career in a school and only occasionally as a research worker in a university. This experience has taught me two things in particular: firstly, that reading failure has usually more than one cause, but that, typically, one factor is mainly responsible; secondly, that almost all reading problems, including those sometimes known as 'dyslexia', will yield to a simple but organised remedial approach.

More important than justifying my competence to write this book, however, is to justify the need for it. You might ask whether there *is* a reading problem and whether anything can be done to help those who are slow readers. I believe there is reasonable cause for concern about children's reading standards and I think that the extent of illiteracy in this country is only gradually being recognised. Newly qualified teachers coming into junior schools are often staggered by the number of children who are unable to read; unfortunately, most colleges of education do not seem to equip their students to deal with the problem. Nor is this lack of technique confined to new teachers; the same strictures apply to a small but significant minority of the established teaching profession.

There are, of course, many schools that do a sound job of teaching reading on a group basis. But they can rarely provide much regular individual teaching, whilst a parent can. I would estimate that ninety per cent of children can be taught to read with occasional help, if an adequate range of reading schemes is used in a school. But of those ninety per cent, thirty per cent would move much more quickly if they received regular and frequent individual tuition. Except in very rare cases, all primary schools have children whom they know they are failing to make literate, and I can confirm from my personal experience how much anxiety they cause to their headteachers and classteachers.

You might feel that the provision of such individual tuition should be the responsibility of the local education authority. Most authorities do in fact have a remedial teaching service consisting of specialist teachers who are not attached to a school and are usually on the staff of the Schools' Psychological Service. Because of the size of the reading problem, it is quite impossible to provide regular individual tuition to all those who might benefit from it. The usual procedure is to reserve the skills of these specialists for children with a severe reading disability.

My assertions about the reading problem need to be backed up by facts and figures. A recent study is very relevant to what I have been saying. Sir Cyril Burt, the first and the most distinguished educational psychologist in this country, in 1969 reported the findings of one of his students who related the norms of comparable tests to those used by Sir Cyril in 1914.[1] Basic attainments, one would think, should be far higher now than they were in those days. Classes then were commonly fifty to sixty strong, and education had been compulsory for only a little over forty years. Taking 1914 as a base of 100, the present-day results were as follows:

Reading Accuracy = 95·4
Reading Comprehension = 99·3
Spelling = 91·1
Mechanical Arithmetic = 92·5
Problem Arithmetic = 96·3

It is easy to pick holes in this kind of comparative study, but I think the results are very sobering indeed.

3

It is not uncommon for as many as one child in five to go on to secondary school, after six years of primary school education, without having reached the generally accepted level of minimal effective literacy (a reading age of around nine years—by which I mean the level of the average nine-year-old). Investigations in Britain and the United States show that approximately ten per cent of children leave school with a reading attainment less than that of the average eleven-year-old.[2, 3] This being the case, it goes without saying that many of the exciting developments in modern education lack a very necessary foundation; almost all of the curricular advances being made add to the demands on the literacy of children. Most of these advances I refer to have come in under the general banner of 'progressive education'. At the same time, I feel that progressive education has been partly responsible for the failure to improve further the reading standards of the school population.

Progressive education, particularly in the primary schools, embodies ideas which psychologists have long advocated: for example, an absence of authoritarian teacher/pupil relationships, motivated learning, and an 'open-ended' learning environment.

Unfortunately, and unnecessarily, a proper balance has not always been achieved, with the result that there has often been insufficient teaching directed to imparting the basic skills of reading and number. This relative absence of direct teaching has been a major tenet for some teachers and educationists, and where this is true the effect on the basic skills has been disastrous. It has also undermined the general effectiveness of the 'open-ended' approach because it has failed to give the children the essential tools of enquiry—literacy and numeracy.

Parents have become increasingly vocal in their

concern about this state of affairs. Sometimes their criticisms have been unthinking and reactionary, but in most cases there has been at least a modicum of justification. All too often, these parents have been fobbed off in one way or another—told that they didn't understand, or were over-anxious (*some* of them were), and so on, and so on. This picture is now changing and, indeed, is changing quite rapidly. Perhaps this book is symptomatic of that change.

We know that reading standards were very low after the Second World War, due, amongst other things, to the interrupted education of evacuees. We know that standards were recovering up to 1964.[2] But evidence is accumulating that the ground regained has been lost.

Some children learn to read with hardly any direct instruction—almost as naturally as they learn to speak. These are a minority: they are usually intellectually bright, though not always, and they are more likely to be girls than boys. Most children need some instruction and a small minority need a good deal.

When should a child start to learn to read? The broad answer is when two conditions are fulfilled:

when the child manifests a desire to do so;

when he has the necessary ability to be successful.

As a general rule, I do not recommend teaching pre-school children to read and I very much suspect the motives of parents who do. Our children start school at a very young age; nowhere else in Europe do children begin school at five years and this does not seem to be to the detriment of their later educational attainments. However, if your child is very keen to read, and I would ask you to make sure that this desire is not just in response to your wish that he or she should do so, and if he is able to fulfil the criteria of ability which I give in the following paragraphs, no harm should be done and possibly some good.

Opinions do vary as to the level of ability necessary to start reading. Downing and Thackray in their recent book on reading readiness[4] point out that it depends on the difficulty of the 'reading' and to what extent the organisation of teaching is helpful. They suggest that under the conditions prevailing in the average English school, five-and-a-half is the normal age for starting to read. My experience agrees with this and I would say that even with an easy, well-organised programme, a *mental age* of five years is the minimum prerequisite. By 'mental age' I mean the ability of the average five-year- old. Even at this level a large minority of five-year-olds starting school do not have the minimum intellectual requirements for starting to read. Equally, a bright four-year-old would have the necessary ability. Remember, however, that this is the *minimum* requirement for the beginning part of learning to read. All children will have reached this level by about seven years chronological age unless they are of extremely limited general intelligence.

I do not recommend that you use an intelligence test to assess your child's level of ability, even assuming that you have access to one. I would not dream of testing my own son. For the purposes of the instruction programme contained in this book, a sophisticated assessment is, in any case, unnecessary. If your child can do the following three things, then it is almost certain that he is ready to begin to learn to read:

speak in sentences, using pronouns correctly;
make a drawing of a man with a fair amount of detail;
copy simple words with reasonable accuracy.

Now we come to the question of the reading methods which might be employed. The main ones are:

1 the *alphabet method*, using the *names* of the letters, e.g. 'c a t' spells 'cat';
2 the *sentence method*—learning to read a whole sentence or phrase at one time;
3 the *'whole-word' method*—learning words as wholes rather than as a combination of sounds (2 and 3 essentially form the 'look-and-say' approach);
4 the *phonic method*—learning the basic sounds (known as 'phonemes') and the letters and combinations of letters (known as graphemes) which represent them, so as to be able to break words down and build them up as recognisable complete words.

There have been fashions in these methods—there is currently an increasing emphasis on phonics—but the 'look-and-say' approach is still strongly established. The alphabet method has not been in wide use since the beginning of the century and is not really a very good method, but it does work and many of our grand-parents or great-grandparents achieved literacy through its aid.

Most successful teachers of reading use a combination of the sentence, whole-word and phonic methods—in that order. They do this, firstly, because it is best to start with something meaningful to children and, secondly, because the sentence method is a little *easier* for a child to grasp than the whole-word method, which is in turn a good deal easier than the phonic method. These 'methods', therefore, need not be considered in opposi-tion to each other but can be seen as stages which blend into one another naturally and allow the child to acquire reading skills in a way suitable to its intel-lectual and conceptual development.

Some teachers start with the phonic method and the children they teach usually manage to learn their letter sounds; what they often cannot do is use them. In my

7

experience these children pick up a whole-word 'sight' vocabulary almost in spite of the method. As a general rule a child needs to reach a mental age of about seven years before he can begin to use phonics *effectively*; by 'effectively' I mean being able to break words down into their component sounds and then to blend the sounds together to make a recognisable word.

Perhaps at this point it is relevant to mention the Initial Teaching Alphabet (i.t.a.). This is often seen as being a method of teaching reading, but it is, in fact, simply a teaching *medium*. It is often assumed that, because i.t.a. provides a different symbol for all the forty-four phonemes (or sound units) in the English language, it necessarily indicates a completely phonic approach. This is not so. What is certainly true is that it makes the phonic approach much easier because it simplifies the process and reduces the learning load. In traditional orthography (t.o.), one phoneme can be represented by several letters or combinations of letters, and conversely one letter or combination of letters can represent several different phonemes.

Where i.t.a. is taught consistently the children have a small advantage over children taught by t.o.. The trouble is that it is not usual to find i.t.a. taught generally even inside one education authority. With parental mobility as common as it is nowadays, children frequently have to switch from i.t.a. to t.o. (or the other way round) at an unsuitable time. I do not think anyone would disagree that this is likely to have an adverse effect on a child's progress in reading. But, of course, this is true of other unstandardised aspects of the curriculum and is the price we pay for the essential freedom we give the teachers in our schools.

If your child has passed the normal age for starting to read (that is, somewhere between his fifth and his seventh birthday), and shows little sign of making a move towards the acquisition of reading skills, the matter may need investigation. Whether your child attends a maintained (local authority) school or not, you can, if you wish, ask for him to be seen by the educational psychologist of the authority in whose area you are resident. This does not have to be done through your child's headteacher, although normally this would be the most sensible and courteous thing to do. Educational psychologists are almost always overworked; headteacher colleagues are aware of this and so try to protect them from 'unnecessary' referrals. But if you are worried you can refer your child to the Schools' Psychological Service whether the headteacher agrees or not; your local education office will give you the address.

In most cases, however, a specialist opinion on a child's failure to read is unnecessary, and the cause or causes are usually a matter of common sense. The three main causes are:

limited ability;

inadequate and/or inappropriate teaching;

poor motivation.

The first means taking care to teach a child at a level where he can learn effectively; there is not much you can do about improving ability and, although you can do something to make reading material easier, in the main the various levels of the teaching of reading must wait on the child's rate of mental development. The second is more easily remediable, even if you have to 'do it yourself' along the lines suggested in this book. The third is usually a response to continued failure; as a general rule, motivation is a product of the proportion of successes to failures. The cure here is to pitch the teaching at a level which guarantees success, and to make a regular habit of reading to the child from books

NOTRE DAME COLLEGE OF EDUCATION.
MO NT PLEASANT, LIVERPOOL L3 5SP

that interest him. Poor motivation is a big handicap in learning to read and with the child of eight years plus who is still not reading, it is almost always the first problem to tackle.

Other, less common, causes of reading failure are:

defects of hearing and vision—particularly long-sightedness (hypermetropia);

specific reading anxiety—marked nervousness and inhibition when the child is faced with reading material;

general emotional disturbance—this affects the efficiency of most learning tasks and, of course, many other aspects of normal functioning;

difficulties more or less specific to reading, for example, poor memory for visual-auditory links, difficulties in maintaining the necessary left to right sequence, reversals or rotations of letters and words, confusion of letter order, and so on (in its *extreme* form this may warrant the diagnostic label of 'dyslexia').

Because of the current state of public interest and misinformation concerning dyslexia (sometimes, inappropriately, called 'word blindness'), I can hardly leave the mention of the term without some elaboration. The first thing I must do is to define what I mean when I use the term, a necessary precaution since its use is extremely variable. In fact, I normally use the term 'specific reading disability', since I consider 'dyslexia' to be a rather question-begging sort of word. I believe that there are abilities relatively specific to reading which are normally distributed throughout the population. Those who are high on these abilities have a specific reading *ability;* those who are low on these abilities have a specific reading *disability*, i.e. they are 'dyslexic'. These abilities, I think, are not necessarily tied to general intelligence—hence the intelligent child who cannot read and hence, also, the intellectually dull child with good mechanical reading ability. Just what these abilities are is the subject of my current research interests.

Currently dyslexia is a cause of some unnecessary referrals to educational psychologists and others whose professional concern it might appear to be. This is partly due to the fervour with which this attractive 'diagnosis' has been seized on by some parents as the reason why their intellectually unexceptional offspring are not making progress. Every psychologist has had some such referrals, but to be honest these are a minority and quite often when parents have thought that their child was suffering from such a reading disability they were right. If your child meets most of the following criteria he may well be dyslexic and referral to your local authority educational psychologist should be considered.

The disability is specific—that is, other attainments, as far as poor reading will allow, are superior.

There are gross and frequent reversals or rotations of letters and words and confused letter order in reading and writing, *which persist after the age of seven or eight years*.

Apparent intelligence is much higher than one would normally associate with the observed level of reading.

Considerable difficulty is experienced in making sense out of printed or written symbols.

There is a history of poor reading and, particularly, weak spelling in other members of the family.

The condition is sometimes accompanied by a degree of ambidexterity and other slight neurological signs such as defective speech and there may be a history of delayed speech or motor development. As one might expect, books by neurologists on dyslexia give considerable prominence to these sorts of characteristics, but their relevance to what is essentially a learning disorder is rather uncertain and some are undoubtedly spurious. I have frequently seen in reports on backward readers reference to their being 'cross-lateral'—that is, they 'sight' with the eye on the opposite side to their preferred hand. Recent research[5] has shown, however, that this is a common condition—one-third of all children are 'cross-lateral'—and that the reading attainment of this group is the same as those who 'sight' with the eye on the *same* side as their preferred hand.

Dyslexia is a serious problem because it can prevent highly intelligent children from achieving as much as they would probably do otherwise. There is, however, no point in trying to diagnose it too early. Anyone going into the reception class of an infants' school would be forgiven for thinking that about thirty per cent of the children were dyslexic. But at this age, and for some time after, children are still maturing neurologically as well as gaining experience in, and understanding of, what are probably to them the mysterious conventions of reading and writing. The point is that these *are* conventions which have to be learnt and it is only from an adult viewpoint that they seem 'natural'. Most children master these basic processes fairly quickly; the dyslexic child is the one who is still struggling at seven plus and has difficulty in learning visually and in maintaining a stable perceptual orientation.

REFERENCES

1 BURT, SIR CYRIL (1969) *Journal of the Association of Educational Psychologists.* Vol. 2; No. 4; p. 8.

2 (1966) *Progress in Reading 1948-1964*. London: Her Majesty's Stationery Office.
3 MONEY, J. (ed.) (1966) *The Disabled Reader*. Baltimore, U.S.A.: The Johns Hopkins University Press.
4 DOWNING, J. A., and THACKRAY, D. V. (1971) *Reading Readiness*. London: University of London Press.
5 CLARK, MARGARET M. (1970) *Reading Difficulties in Schools*. Harmondsworth: Penguin Books.

# Section One

Although there is nothing novel or revolutionary about the contents of this book, I do not know of any other specific programme about the teaching of reading for parents. My especial contribution I feel is to have organised the teaching according to the findings of what psychologists call 'learning theory'. In short, I have tried to design the programme for the most economic and effective learning.

Learning theory is the general title applied to the psychological research into how learning takes place. It is perhaps the most important subject in psychology because most human behaviour, including emotional behaviour, is *learnt*. Learning can be a very haphazard process; the application of the lessons of learning theory help us to make it less so.

The main principles from this body of knowledge which I have employed are as follows:

1 spaced learning is more effective than massed learning, so a little and often is the best rule;

2 an organised presentation of the material to be learnt is more effective than a haphazard presentation;

3 meaningful material is learnt more rapidly than unmeaningful material so we start with sentences tied to pictures and not with relatively meaningless phonic units;

4 reinforcement (that is, reward) strengthens learning, so reward judiciously, particularly in the beginning stages, by verbal praise or something more tangible— in time the child's own success will become sufficient reward;

5 'overlearning'—continuing to learn past the point of immediate recall—is necessary for 'firm' learning;
6 learning is more effective if the material is broken down into small, but clearly related, stages;
7 breaks between learning sessions enable what has been learnt to become 'fixed'.

By putting these principles into practice in the programme I have designed, I expect to increase the probability of you and your child succeeding in this joint venture.

The first major goal is to give your child a reasonably substantial 'sight' vocabulary—by this, I mean around 150-200 words he will recognise on sight. A recognition vocabulary of this size will take him up to a reading age of about seven years. The rate at which it will be achieved will depend on the age and ability of your child. An intelligent eight-year-old who is a retarded reader should make up the ground quicker, provided the reasons for the retardation are relatively uncomplicated, than a seven-year-old who is intellectually just about ready to start. Your child will, in any case, soon show you his own learning pace.

You do not start with any published reading books, nor are these the mainstay of the learning programme. Instead the child, with your help, makes his own reading books, writing about things he knows and using the words he understands.

The first step will be to make a reading book with about twenty-five different words in it. This will be followed by eight books with about fifteen new words in each. The books after the first one have fewer *new* words because many of the common words will be repetitions of those in the first book.

The number of words covered in each book may seem small to an adult, but they are quite enough for a child

L. I. H. E.

THE BECK

who is beginning to learn to read. If a child is to learn to recognise a word and retain that recognition he will probably need to meet it in a variety of ways a minimum of thirty times, and sometimes much more often. If you think this initial goal is unambitious, let me say that it is not an uncommon experience for me to see children of eight or nine, of normal intelligence, who can recognise no more than half a dozen words in the English language.

The sessions vary considerably in the length of time they will require—from ten to thirty minutes. This difference is deliberate and is designed for maximum effectiveness. Do not try to give a lesson *every* day— leave the weekends free and observe the other breaks recommended. A reasonable passage of time is necessary for learnt skills to integrate and develop; the main danger at this level is the desire to 'telescope' the process.

Don't worry about interruptions caused by holidays, visits, and so on, provided they are not too protracted —just carry on from where you left off. And remember that although regular sessions are important, to push on with a lesson when either you or your child is not in the mood is asking for trouble. Similarly, if he has a favourite television programme at his usual lesson time, postpone the lesson until later (or bring it forward). Never make the instruction sessions act as a depriver; if you do, you'll make them a punishment and defeat your aim.

## The first twenty-five words

You will need a fair-sized plain drawing book for the child and a small lined notebook for yourself in which to keep a record of the words used. In this notebook you will need to list each different word and, as words start to repeat, their frequency and the book(s) in which they appear, e.g.

the ~~HHt-HHt~~ ~~HHt-HHt~~ III

    (Books 1, 2, 3, 4, 5, 6, 7, 8, 9)

dog IIII

    (Books 1, 4, 7)

This will enable you to locate words, if necessary, and also give you an idea of the coverage the words have received.

You start by suggesting to the child that he does a drawing. What the drawing is about doesn't matter, but most children will need some suggestions to get them started. The drawings in the book don't need to be on the same theme—except in a very broad sense this is impossible anyway with young children.

The child should be encouraged whilst he is making the drawing and praised for it afterwards. Then you

ask what it is, or what it is about and from what the child says, *using his own words*, you devise a suitable description. You should not make the description longer than five words and three or four words is most satisfactory; be sure to include a verb if you can.

Let us assume that you and your child agree that a suitable descriptive sentence for the first drawing is 'My dad in the garden.' You print this under the picture, using lower case (small) letters and capitals where appropriate, and taking care not to make them too small. Read out what you have written, pointing to each word as you say it, and then ask the child to copy it underneath. Having read out loud what he has written, ask him to do the same, making sure that he points to each word in turn. Correct him if necessary, but once he can say it reasonably finish the session. One session like this is quite enough for one day.

The following sessions should be the same as this one —a drawing and an accompanying sentence. At the beginning of these subsequent sessions, however, the *previous day's* sentence should be read first, corrected if necessary, but not laboured. Continue these sessions until your record shows that you have around twenty-five different words. This will normally take about ten daily sessions to achieve. We will call this Reading Book 1A.

We will assume for the sake of example that the first reading book and your record contain the material set out on the next page. I have done this to give you an impression of what you will have to work on in the remaining sessions of this first part of the programme. It is not supposed to be a model to which you and your child have to conform; the reading book you will make together will be personal and unique—and therein lies its particular value as a basis for further teaching.

## Example of sentences in Reading Book 1A

1 My dad in the garden.
2 My dog is big.
3 A lorry in the road.
4 Our cat eats fish.
5 My sister is little.
6 My new bike is red.
7 I run to school.
8 My dad has a bike.
9 My sister eats sweets.

## Word content of Reading Book 1A

| A | a 11 | J | | | school 1 |
|---|---|---|---|---|---|
| B | big 1 | K | | | sweets 1 |
| | bike 11 | L | lorry 1 | T | the 11 |
| C | cat 1 | | little 1 | | to 1 |
| D | dad 11 | M | my 111 | U | |
| | dog 1 | N | new 1 | V | |
| E | eats 11 | O | our 1 | W | |
| F | fish 1 | P | | X | |
| G | garden 1 | Q | | Y | |
| H | has 1 | R | road 1 | Z | |
| I | in 11 | | run 1 | | |
| | I 1 | | red 1 | | |
| | is 111 | S | sister 11 | | |

## Sessions One to Ten (approximately)

The making of the first reading book in the manner I have described will have taken you about a couple of weeks, assuming you have given your child a break at weekends. As you can see from my example on the previous page, we call this first book Reading Book 1A.

The big temptation is to try to get this first book done very quickly, but, as I said earlier, the intervals between the sessions are very important and facilitate learning in all its aspects. I cannot repeat too often that to try to gallop your child through this course will almost certainly end in disaster.

## Session Eleven
This session simply consists of going through the book reading each sentence. Correct any errors, but don't labour them; a couple of attempts at each sentence is adequate.

## Session Twelve
In preparation for this session you will need to write each sentence without any illustration in another book; this can be made of sheets of paper stapled together. We will call this Reading Book 1B. Write each sentence on a separate page and in a straight line. This time you

I run to school

My dog is big

Our cat eats fish

My dad has a bike

My new bike is red

A lorry in the road

My dad in the garden

My sister eats sweets

My sister is little

get your child to read the first four or five sentences in turn, copying each one underneath and reading it again.

## Session Thirteen
The same as the previous session, but work on the remaining four or five sentences.

## Session Fourteen
You will need to make sentence cards this time, each sentence being written on a separate strip of card. Cover each sentence in Reading Book 1A with a strip of paper hinged at the top with Sellotape so that it can be lifted to read the sentence underneath (see page 21).

Open the book at the first picture, spread the sentence cards around and say, 'Which one goes with this picture?' If your child picks the wrong one say, 'No, try again.' If he is wrong a second time say, 'No, I think it's this one, let's check and see.' Ask him to lift up the flap and check the sentence card with the sentence on the page; then he reads it. Most children find this a particularly enjoyable game and if they have gone through it fairly quickly, you can let them try it again. But twice is certainly enough.

## Session Fifteen
For this and the next session you will need to make big word cards (each letter about an inch high), one for each *different* word in the book. In the unlikely event of any of the sentences containing the same word twice, you will need an extra card for that word.

Open the picture book (Reading Book 1A) at the first page, spread the word cards around and then

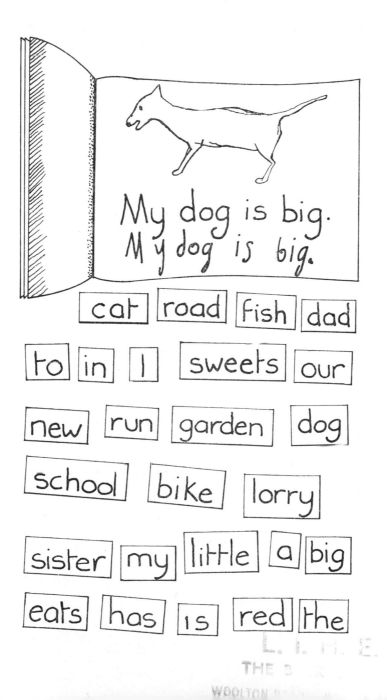

My dog is big.
My dog is big.

cat road fish dad

to in I sweets our

new run garden dog

school bike lorry

sister my little a big

eats has is red the

L. I. H. E.
THE D
WOOLTON

pointing to the sentence say, 'Watch me, I'm going to make this with the word cards.' As you select them, put each word against its counterpart in the sentence before putting it in the correct order underneath. When you've done that, ask the child to read the sentence pointing to each word in turn. Then ask him to shut his eyes, replace the word cards with the others which are scattered around and say, 'Open your eyes; now you do it.' If he selects a wrong card say, 'Is it the same as this one?' (pointing to the correct word in the sentence). If it seems clear that he is unable to pick the correct word fairly quickly, do it for him; in either case he is asked to read the sentence through before going on to the next page.

In this session you should cover half of the sentences in the book, but remember that you only demonstrate the first one.

## Session Sixteen
As Session 15, but work on the remaining sentences.

At this point break off instruction for a full week. Make this a complete break, with no attempt at revision or practice.

By this time your child will almost certainly be reading the sentences in his reading book fluently and you might think that this is the time for the next book. In this you are quite wrong: the learnings are not yet fixed and further consolidation is crucial. In any case, your child is learning more than just to recognise a few words, he is learning important general principles and these require a chance to grow.

## Session Seventeen

A 'flash card' session: take the word cards you have already made and holding each one up in turn ask, 'What does this say?' Don't wait more than five seconds for a response and if your child hasn't read it by then put it on one side. I think you will soon see what I meant when I said that the learnings were not firmly established! You will probably notice that the nouns which occurred less frequently in the book are not necessarily the least well learnt. This is because they are the most *meaningful* words—they are the *names* of things.

When you've gone through all the words in this fashion, take the flash cards which your child could not recognise, and holding each one up in turn, say the word yourself and get him to repeat it. Do this once only.

## Session Eighteen

This session requires a child's blackboard or a large piece of hardboard and some chalk. Taking the word cards that were not recognised at the previous session (or any others that seem 'weak'), hold each one up in turn and ask your child to read it. If he can't, say it for him and get him to repeat it. In either case you then say, 'Now you copy it on your board.' This done, he reads the word again before you show him the next card.

## Session Nineteen

This time you will need to have made a set of alphabet cards, one for each letter of the alphabet. Each card should have the letter in lower case form (not capitals). At this point we are going to introduce the very beginnings of phonics, what I call 'initial letter phonics'.

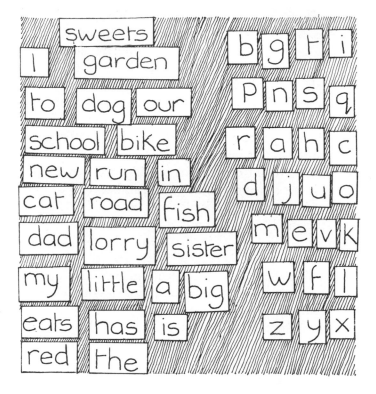

This is not of key importance at this stage of the programme, but it is important that we should do a little groundwork now. Do not try to teach your child all of the *different* sounds made by the *same* letters at this stage; some of them are of little importance anyway. All you need to do is to provide a little practice in helping your child to discriminate the initial letter sounds of the words in his current reading book. Spread over the whole series of reading books he will be making, this will provide him with plenty of practice and make a useful bridge to the later, more intensively phonic, part of this instruction programme.

You will need quite a lot of table-space for this session. Spread the word cards around on one side and the alphabet cards on the other side; make sure the alphabet cards are not in alphabetical order. Pick up an alphabet card which is the initial letter of more than one word in the reading book (in the examples I have given it could be the letter '*b*'), then say, 'This says *buh*' (making sure you say the *sound* of the letter not its 'name', in this instance *buh* not *bee*). Saying a sound so that the child can see its significance as part of a word is not as easy as it might seem, because in trying to say it separately it is difficult to avoid adding an additional, distorting, sound. The example I have given shows this! The secret is to produce the sound quietly and 'on the breath', cutting it short at the right moment. You won't find this difficult, after a little practice, but it is important to master the technique yourself, since you have to pass it on to your child. Much of the difficulty that children experience when they come to blend sounds together is due to the fact that they have learnt distorted letter sounds in the first place.

To continue: after saying the sound in the correct fashion yourself tell the child, 'Now *you* say what it says.' Make the child repeat it after you two or three times, emphasising the technique of making the correct sound. Pointing to the word cards scattered around ask, 'Can you see any words that start with *b*?' If your child selects a wrong word, put the alphabet card against the initial letter of the word and ask, 'Is that the same?' Most children can do this fairly easily after one or two corrections, but if your child doesn't seem to get the idea, pick a word out for him. In either case, when the word has been selected, ask your child to say the sound and then to say the word that begins with the sound; do this two or three times for each word and letter.

Sometimes, of course, your child will pick out a word that begins with the same letter as the alphabet card but in fact makes a different sound, such as the letter 't' and the word 'the'. When this happens just say to your child, 'That's a special word; it's one that likes to be different. There are some words like that and I will tell you about them when we meet them.' *Do not try to teach your child exceptions to the rules at this stage.*

If you cover half the initial letter sounds included in the current reading book that will be sufficient for this session.

## Session Twenty

The same as the previous session, but go through the remainder of the letter sounds.

## Session Twenty-one

You will almost certainly have played 'lotto', 'housey-housey' or 'bingo' at some time and you will know that each player has a card with numbers on it which are covered with counters, or crossed out, as they are 'called' by one of the players. Obviously, you can do exactly the same thing with words and in this session we are going to play 'word lotto'.

Using your basic twenty-five words, make three lotto cards with eight or nine different words on each, as shown in the illustration. Then make *small* individual cards, one for each word, and the same size as the words on the lotto cards. The caller *says* the words, but does not *show* them. This can be played with just two of you, yourself acting as caller to begin with, but having one of the lotto cards as well to make a game of it. It does, however, work better with three people playing

| a | cat | eats |
|---|---|---|
| has | is | my |
| road | sister | the |

| big | dad | fish |
|---|---|---|
| in | lorry | new |
| run | school | to |

| bike | dog | garden |
|---|---|---|
| I | little | our |
| red | sweets | //////// |

it and this third person should be another adult, or an older child—not one close enough in age to be in competition with the child under instruction.

This is a great game for improving word recognition and is usually much enjoyed by children. The child you are teaching will almost certainly want to have a turn at being the caller and it won't matter if you have to give a little help over recognising words. Because this kind of word game is popular, the danger is that you might overdo it; about three games in one session is ample. If your child is left with an appetite for more that is all to the good.

## Session Twenty-two

Read through Reading Book 1A (the one with the pictures and the sentences) and Reading Book 1B (the one with sentences only). Any sentences misread should be repeated once, but make it an easy session.

## Session Twenty-three

Word-matching: use the lotto cards and the caller's small individual word cards. Give your child one of the lotto cards and spread the word cards around it. Point to a word on the lotto card and say, 'You see this word, I want you to find it in the words around here and put it on top of the word on the card.' Children sometimes make a slow start on this one, but move rapidly when they get the idea. Use all three lotto cards in turn.

## Session Twenty-four

For this session you will need to make a new reading book which we shall call Book 1C, using the same words but forming new sentences. Write one sentence on each

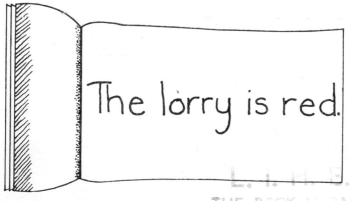

The lorry is red.

L. . . . .
THE B CK L RARY
WOOLTON ROAD, . L16 8

page. This is not really very difficult and it does not matter how often you use each word. Reading the words correctly in this rearranged form is an important test of your child's grasp of the words which are being learnt.

Encourage your child to read the book through fairly quickly. Do this two or three times, so that a satisfactory level of fluency is achieved.

Below there is an illustration of rearranged sentences, using the words in the previous examples I have given.

## Example of rearranged sentences in Reading Book 1 C

1 A cat is in our garden.
2 I run in the road.
3 A big dog eats the fish.
4 My dad is in the lorry.
5 I run to my dad.
6 Our cat is little.
7 My sister has a bike.
8 My school is new.
9 Our dog eats sweets.
10 The lorry is red.

## Session Twenty-five

'Initial letter phonics' as in Sessions 19 and 20 (pages 26-9), but cover the whole range of initial letter sounds in the one session.

## Session Twenty-six

Word lotto.

## Session Twenty-seven

Sentence building—as in Sessions 15 and 16 (pages 22-4), but use Book 1C and go through the whole book in one session.

## Session Twenty-eight

Phonic 'I Spy': this is an excellent game for building up the discrimination of initial letter sounds. Use objects around the room and 'plant' suitable ones if necessary. Remember that when you use the traditional formula of 'I spy with my little eye something beginning with . . .' you say the *sound* of the initial letter and not its name. Explain the game and 'spy' two or three things for each initial letter sound you have covered so far. Don't let your child search too long, and if you have to say the word, emphasise the initial sound.

## Session Twenty-nine

Word lotto.

## Session Thirty

This is the final session of the first stage and not an arduous one. Test your child's word recognition by using flash cards, holding them up for not more than three seconds. Make a note of the words failed.

This last session should be taken lightly, but it is a significant test of progress and predictive of probable future success. If fewer than four words are failed on this 'speed' test of recognition then the programme is

NOTRE DAME COLLEGE OF EDUCATION,
MOUNT PLEASANT, LIVERPOOL L3 5SP

suited to your child and future progress should be good. More failures than this indicate a need for caution and it might be advisable to delay moving on to another book for about six months. However, I should hope that you would not have allowed your child to struggle through this beginning part of the programme if it was obviously too much for him. Whatever you do, don't go back to the beginning of a book you've just worked through; that would be very demoralising.

In any case, take a two-week break before starting on the next book. During that period any words failed in the final session should be written out on large cards and hung up round the house—behind the lavatory door is a good place! The point is to make a bit of a joke of it, so hang them on door-knobs, coat-hooks, and so on. Just say, 'When you think you know one of them, bring it to me.' This may seem a little obsessional, but it has the virtue of thoroughness, which children appreciate. But don't overdo it—100 per cent retention is not all that important, and if you make it your short-term object it may defeat your long-term goal.

The next eight books should be added in the same fashion, following the programme outlined in this first stage. Do not try to add more than fifteen *new* words each time—that really is ample—and in each stage concentrate on these fifteen new words and let the ones that have occurred before take care of themselves. This last point is very important because to be effective, learning must be fairly narrowly focussed. The only exception to this should be in the final flash card session when the words from the previous stage should be included. If any of these words are 'failed' they should be followed up, as I have suggested, during the fortnight's 'between the stages' rest period.

Keep a record of the fifteen or so new words inside

the front cover of your child's reading book, apart from adding them to your cumulative vocabulary list.

Part of the reinforcement of success for a child is that he is given 'real' books to read. At the end of this section I list three groups of reading books, the groups being graded according to the reading skill they require. Most educational booksellers will have some of these in stock but you may have to order them specially. All of the books are suitable for children of junior school age, but obviously your child will develop preferences. If you try a number of different ones to begin with you will be able to follow through the series that seem most successful.

The books in Group One are suitable for children who have completed Books Two and Three of our programme; Group Two should be left until after Books Four, Five and Six; and Group Three until after Books Seven, Eight and Nine.

Choose two or three of these to be read during the 'rest period'. Help your child with unfamiliar words and encourage him to use the first letter and make a guess from the context. Don't bother about getting him to learn them; the reading of these 'real' books should be divorced from the atmosphere of instruction in reading. By the time he is reading books from the Second Group you will probably find that your child is making reasonable guesses at unfamiliar words anyway. One further point: make this a real 'rest period' by reading *to* him more than usual.

If we assume that your child has coped successfully with the first reading book he made in this first section you may, nonetheless, wonder whether the particular words he has learnt are the most important. There is one overwhelming answer to this—namely that the words were important to *him* and came from his own vocabulary. You may think, however, that he should have started with more common words. There are words which occur very frequently in the English language and in that sense these are the most important, but they will come in during the course of this programme just because they are so common. Starting to learn to read is not like starting at the beginning of a line; it is more like breaking into a circle. Because of this it is not so important where you begin as how you proceed. To return to the idea of the circle, without direction it is easy to lose your way once you are inside.

You might ask, nonetheless, whether you should not start with small words. In fact, small words are not necessarily easily learnt, often because, being prepositions, conjunctions, and so on, they have little meaning attached to them. Nouns familiar to the child are likely to be learnt more easily. Even if you concede this you may still feel that you ought to start with common everyday nouns. Actually there are few really common nouns and research shows that nouns tend to be fairly specific. But in any case, in starting to learn to read a child is learning much more than just to 'bark at print' —he is learning a new kind of skill. The link between the spoken and the printed or written word may seem automatic to an adult, but a child may not be aware of the real nature of the relationship between the sounds that come out of his mouth and the series of black marks on paper. Learning to read is an important step forward in a child's language development because it carries the process of abstraction one stage further: he has learnt to 'decode' meaning from combinations of sounds in spoken language; reading means that he first has to 'decode' the sounds from a mysterious convention of marks on paper.

# Recommended reading books (Section One)

## GROUP ONE

| Series | Books | Author | Publisher |
|---|---|---|---|
| Keywords Reading Scheme (Ladybird) | 1a, 1b 2a, 2b 3a, 3b | W. Murray | Wills and Hepworth |
| Griffin Readers | Pre-readers 1-4 | S. McCullagh | E. J. Arnold |
| Adventures in Reading | 1, 2, 2a | G. Keir | Oxford University Press |
| Oxford Colour Reading Books | (1) A-F | C. Carver and C. H. Stowasser | Oxford University Press |

## GROUP TWO

| Series | Books | Author | Publisher |
|---|---|---|---|
| Keywords Reading Scheme (Ladybird) | 4a, 4b | W. Murray | Wills and Hepworth |
| Griffin Readers | 1, 2 | S. McCullagh | E. J. Arnold |
| Adventures in Reading | 3, 3a | G. Keir | Oxford University Press |
| Oxford Colour Reading Books | (2) A-F | C. Carver and C. H. Stowasser | Oxford University Press |

| | | | |
|---|---|---|---|
| Racing to Read | 1-4 | A. E. Tansley and R. H. Nicholls | E. J. Arnold |

## GROUP THREE

| Series | Books | Author | Publisher |
|---|---|---|---|
| Keywords Reading Scheme (Ladybird) | 5a, 5b | W. Murray | Wills and Hepworth |
| Griffin Readers | 3, 4 | S. McCullagh | E. J. Arnold |
| Adventures in Reading | 4, 4a | G. Keir | Oxford University Press |
| Oxford Colour Reading Books | (3) A-F | C. Carver and C. H. Stowasser | Oxford University Press |
| Racing to Read | 5-8 | A. E. Tansley and R. H. Nicholls | E. J. Arnold |

## Supplementary list of reading books (*Group Four*)

These books are of approximately the same level of difficulty as those in Group Three. They will prove useful if your child demands more reading books at this stage, as he well might, or if you decide to delay starting

Section Two of the teaching programme. Similarly, if you are intending to start at Section Two, omitting Section One, the books at this level will provide a useful 'limbering up' exercise, as well as giving you some idea as to whether it is really wise to miss out Section One in your child's case.

| Series | Books | Author | Publisher |
|--------|-------|--------|-----------|
| Dragon Books | B1, B2, B3, B4, B5 | S. McCullagh | E. J. Arnold |
| Gay Way Series | Blue Book | E. R. Boyce | Macmillan |
| Mike and Mandy | 4, 5, 6 | M. Durward | Nelson |
| Royal Road Readers | 3, 4 | J. C. Daniels and Hunter Diack | Chatto and Windus |
| Through the Rainbow | Green (1-3) Blue (1-3) | E. S. Bradburne | Schofield and Sims |

L. I. H. E.
THE BOOK LIBRARY
WOOLTON ROAD, L16 8ND

# Section Two

We can reasonably assume that, having worked through the vocabulary of nine reading books of his own making and also having read about a dozen conventional reading books, your child will have, as an absolute minimum, a word recognition vocabulary of between 150 and 200 words. In all probability the number will be much greater than this. In addition he will have a firm grasp of the common phonic equivalents of most of the letters of the alphabet. These acquired skills, combined with adequate general intellectual development, will enable him to make use of the more sophisticated phonic skills which are necessary if he is to read the very large vocabulary contained in even the most ordinary 'proper' books.

In other words, he must now go on to learn those combinations of letters which either represent individual sounds or two sounds blended together so that they are, in effect, inseparable. Most of these combinations of letters are known as 'digraphs' and for the sake of simplicity I shall use the term to describe them all, except for the self-explanatory group of 'word endings'. Examples of digraphs are shown in such words as: *sh*ip, ri*ch*, lo*ud*; examples of common word endings are: kick*ed*, pa*ge*, be*ing*.

It is possible, but unlikely, that your child, having completed the first stage of building up a sight vocabulary may not be ready to pass on immediately to the second stage of acquiring the more complex phonic skills. You will find this out in the early stages of this section. If it seems clear that the lessons are too difficult for him, postpone the transition for six months and concentrate on providing plenty of reading books at a suitable level of difficulty, e.g. from the books in Group Three of the last Section (page 38) or the Supplementary List, Group Four (page 39).

The great value of phonics is that it enables a child to break into unfamiliar words by sounding out the word in its basic phonic units and then attempting to blend these together to make a word recognisable in his experienced vocabulary. The importance of this skill, when it is stated in this fashion, is so evident that you may well ask why reading is not taught in this way from the beginning. I did deal with this question briefly on pages 7 and 8 but the arguments are worth elaborating here. Firstly, for children beginning to read it is important to start with the nearest meaningful point and the grapheme (the printed or written equivalent of a phoneme, or unit of speech-sound) is really quite a long way from the spoken language; meaningful sentences are correspondingly much nearer. Secondly, phonics is intellectually difficult, and by this, of course, I mean difficult for young children. Not only is there a large number of different ways of representing the speech-sounds in writing so that there is a lot to learn, but also the system is qualified by irregularities and exceptions which make demands upon judgement and reasoning. Because of this it is generally considered that a mental age of about seven years is necessary before phonics at anything approaching this level can be effectively employed. Thirdly, and this is always a danger with a phonic approach, it can lead to a very laboured and unfluent style of reading; children who start by reading 'at sight' are more likely to establish as a fundamental the habit of fluency.

There are forty-four basic phonemes or speech-sound units in the English language and our traditional alphabet is only a very modest attempt to produce graphemic equivalents. Pitman's Augmented Roman Alphabet,

41

now known as the Initial Teaching Alphabet (i.t.a.), provides a different graphic symbol for each separate phoneme. Teaching a child phonic values in i.t.a. is very much easier than teaching them in traditional orthography. Furthermore, the child who has learnt a sight vocabulary in i.t.a. will often have discerned its phonic regularity and so learnt most of the graphic-phonic connections. This 'artificial' regularity does in fact seem to facilitate the transfer back to the more uneven regularities of traditional orthography and this teaches us something of great value for learning phonics in t.o.— namely, that it is more important to concentrate on the *general rules* than the exceptions to those rules. When you are working through this section of the programme dealing with phonics, by all means mention the exceptions and clarify them, but keep the general rules in the centre of your attention.

Before we proceed with the actual phonics programme it is important to consider exactly what a child has to learn.

1 He must know the sounds made by the individual letters (with variations)—in this programme this skill will have been largely acquired in the previous section.
2 He has to recognise when combinations of two or three letters make a special kind of sound.
3 He has to be aware of the syllabic structure of words.
4 He has to be able to blend the sounds together and recognise the whole word.

The first part is really not very difficult and if this were the only phonic skill required, despite the fact that some letters stand for several sounds, phonics would be quite easy. The discrimination of digraphs and the perception of the syllabic structure of words, however, need to be high-lighted for most children at this stage; equally, the knack of blending from a number of separate phonemes and allowing for the consequent distortion needs both help and practice.

The discrimination of digraphs seems to be easily acquired by a number of children, but for a large minority this is not the case and it is certainly true to say that the 'phonic barrier' is the hurdle which has defeated most failed readers. By focussing on a small number of these digraphs at a time and 'overlearning' them, the special discrimination that they require will gradually become more fluent and apparently 'automatic'. However, before we go on to this, the most difficult part of the programme, we must first have practice in sounding out and blending at a simple level. We do this by concentrating on words of one syllable which contain no digraphs.

## Session One

Revision of single-letter sounds: using individual letter cards (and omitting 'q' and 'x'), run through the basic sounds, first by holding each one up in turn (not in alphabetical order) and asking your child to give the sounds; and then by spreading them all out on a table and saying, 'Give me the ones I call out.' Go through them all, calling them out at random, and return the cards he picks up. Make a note of any sounds failed in either approach, as these must be tackled right away.

Providing a blackboard, or piece of hardboard, and chalk say, 'We're going to deal with those sounds you're not sure of. I'll call them out, together with some of the sounds you do know, and you try to write them down. If you can't I'll do it for you.' Call them out quickly, moving from one sound to another but focussing on those which have caused difficulty. Clean the board frequently so as not to provide clues to recognition.

## Session Two
Phonic 'I Spy' as in Session 28 of the previous Section
(page 33).


## Session Three
Phonic dictation: this is essentially the same as the latter
part of Session One. Going through all the sounds call
them out fairly quickly, but judge the exact pace to suit
your child. Although it is satisfactory to ask him to write
them down on paper, it always seems to work better with
blackboard and chalk. Any letters that he can't repro-
duce from their sounds you should write for him, getting
him to repeat the sound. As it becomes clear which letters
these are, focus on them in the latter part of the session.
This session is a good test of whether he knows his sounds.
If you have worked through Section One of this programme with him and find that at this stage he has
difficulty in reproducing the written equivalents of the
sounds, you should postpone going on to the rest of the
programme. If you have started with this Section, you
can repeat these first three sessions; if your child is still
in difficulties you should start with Section One (see
page 14).

## *The Wordmaker*
Explain to your child that you are going to make words
using a special machine called the Wordmaker and that
he will have to read the words by sounding all the letters
out as you go along. The Wordmaker, as the accompanying illustration shows, is a piece of cardboard approximately six inches square with three pairs of parallel slots
one inch wide through which are pulled, from top to
bottom, three strips of card just under an inch in width.
These three strips of card carry a series of individual

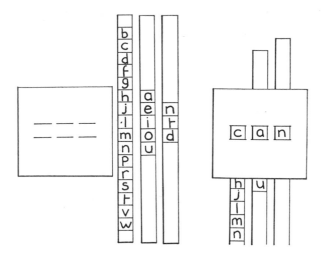

letters, each being allowed a one inch 'box' so that they
will neatly fit the 'window' between the slots. The first
(left-hand) strip contains the following initial consonants in the given order: b, c, d, f, g, h, j, l, m, n, p, r, s,
t, v, w. The second (middle) strip bears the five vowels:
a, e, i, o, u. The end strip has just three terminal consonants: n, t, d.

Tell your child that you are going to make the words
by pulling the strips to show different letters in each of
the three windows. Explain that during each session
the middle letter, which is called a vowel, will be the
same and so will the last letter. Add that the last letter
and also the first letters of the words you will make are
called consonants. Say that there are only five vowels in
the alphabet and that each of them will come up in the
middle window of the Wordmaker in due course. Point
out that although you will be making little words with
just three letters in them, all big words are made up of
little words like that and these little words are called

syllables. Tell him that if he can read the syllables, later on he will be able to read the big words by adding the syllables together.

You will, of course, need to reiterate these points many times during the following sessions; I summarise them here merely for convenience.

## Sessions Four-Eighteen

For each session the vowel/terminal consonant combination remains the same and they are sounded out in conjunction with each of the sixteen initial consonants. Some of these, of course, will not make words but they will all provide sounding out and blending practice. Discriminating those which make real words is part of the exercise. Each time ask your child, when he has sounded out and blended, 'Does that make a word?' If you agree that it does, ask him to write it down before you go on to the next combination. Sometimes the words produced will be phonically correct, but incorrectly spelt—for example 'wot'. When these occur, explain that many words are not spelt as they sound and write out the correct spelling, emphasising that although they are pronounced in the same way the correct spelling is not the obvious one.

When you have worked through the sixteen combinations, take the list he has made and, without his being able to see the words, sound each one out and ask him to say which word it makes.

Fifteen sessions of doing this may seem rather a lot in sequence, but in fact children enjoy it very much because of the simple apparatus and it does establish very fluent basic phonic habits.

# Section Three

As you will have found in the previous stage, it is not very difficult to teach children the sounds made by individual letters even when one letter can be sounded in two or three different ways. But children do find it hard to grasp the idea that certain letters together may make a special sound of their own; the child who is slow in learning to read will probably not make these discriminations unless we teach him to do so. In this part of the section, therefore, we are going to work on the acquisition of those sounds which are represented by more than one letter. These combinations of two or three letters are known as 'digraphs' and there are somewhere around 250 of them in the English language. It would be tedious as well as uneconomic to learn each one; in any case, some of them are more or less similar, others are uncommon, and any child being taught systematically will gradually be able to pick out even those which he has not actually learnt.

We are going to concentrate on fifty of these digraphs and a number of word endings, tackling them eight or nine at a time rather in the way that we dealt with different words in the previous section when we were building up a sight vocabulary. The list on the next page divides the digraphs and word endings into the seven groups we shall work through. The lists that follow provide (in most cases) twelve fairly common words for each different digraph or word ending; these will prove useful as source material during the instruction sessions.

# Digraphs and word endings
## Group One
EE  SH  CH  ER  AY  CK  TH  $\boxed{-\text{ING}}$

## *Group Two*
OO\*  EA\*  OW\*  AI  LL  ST  GR  $\boxed{\text{vowel}+\text{E}}$

## *Group Three*
OA  AR\*  OR\*  AW  OU  BR  CL  $\boxed{-\text{LE}}$

## *Group Four*
SP  BL  IR  SC  TR  CR  FL  $\boxed{-\text{GE}}$

## *Group Five*
SK  PL  TW  SL  PR  FR  SM  $\boxed{-\text{Y}}$

## *Group Six*
GL  WH  UR  DR  SW  SN  QU  $\boxed{-\text{ED}}$

## *Group Seven*
OY  PH  AU  OI  EW  KN  WR  IGH  $\boxed{-\text{ION}}$ and $\boxed{-\text{OUS}}$

The word endings are boxed in.

## Group One

**EE**
feed    seed    see    eel    keen    heel    feel    bee
weed    deep    week    beef

**SH**
shop    ship    shot    cash    dish    shed    rush    wish
fish    ash    rash    shut

**CH**
chop    chin    chat    chip    rich    such    inch
punch    catch    match    ditch    kitchen

\* Starred digraphs represent *two* phonemes, e.g. t*ea* and h*ea*d.

**ER**

| her | winner | runner | master | after | sister |
|-----|--------|--------|--------|-------|--------|
| term | ever | dinner | winter | number | summer |

**AY**

hay   say   day   lay   away   may   ray   pay
bay   gay   way   repay

**CK**

pick   dock   tick   lock   muck   back   sack
neck   kick   sick   duck   sock

**TH**

that   this   with   than   then   them   ('hard' th)
thank   thin   think   thug   thump   thud   ('soft' th)

**–*ING***

being   sitting   hitting   running   having   king
sing   ring   adding   rubbing   wing   missing

## Group Two

**OO**

tool   too   hoot   loot   root   pool
wood   wool   book   good   cook   foot

**EA**

tea   seat   read   hear   pea   fear
head   dead   deaf   meant   heaven   leant

**OW**

cow   now   town   how   down   owl
bow   sow   tow   low   own   bowl   (the first two of these
can also be pro-
nounced in the same
way as the previous
six)

**AI**

rain   main   pail   rail   hail   pain   faint   nail
tail   paid   laid   wait

**LL**

bill   ill   sell   bell   full   doll

fall  hall  all  tall  ball  call (note that 'a' before 'll'
                                  does not make its usual
                                  sound as do the other
                                  vowels)

ST
stop  stand  stamp  last  cost  fast  fist  list
cast  step  dust  best

GR
grip  grab  grand  grass  grin  grasp  grunt
gravel  grandpa  grandma  grit  grim

*vowel* + *E*
gate  cake  same  five  wide       (explain that the
mine  hope  rose  hole  tune       'e' at the end
use  rude                          usually  makes
                                   the vowel before
                                   say its 'name')

## Group Three
OA
boat  coat  oats  loaf  load  road  goal  goat
toad  loan  oak  soap

AR
art  card  arm  mark  car  farm
war  warm  warden  ward  warp  ('ar' after 'w'
                               pronounced as
                               'or')

OR
or  worn  sort  for  pork  form
worm  word  work  worse  world ('or' pronounced as
worth                          'ur' after 'w' ex-
                               cept in 'worn')

AW
saw  lawn  law  fawn  jaw  paw  raw  yawn
dawn  awful  awning  pawn

OU
loud  out  mound  foul  about  round  pound
sound  found  hound  count  bout

50

**BR**

brim  brand  brass  brag  brat  brink  brisk
brown  broke  brook  British  bring

**CL**

clap  clip  class  cliff  club  clinic  clump
cling  close  cloth  clown  clean

**-LE**

bottle  cattle  middle  apple  handle  kettle
puddle  bundle  rattle  settle  paddle  muddle

## Group Four

**SP**

spin  spit  spot  lisp  span  spank  speed
spell  spend  spill  splendid  split

**BL**

blank  blade  blanket  bleed  bless  blond  blot
blow  blunt  blush  blue  blind

**IR**

dirt  bird  sir  firm  fir  girl  first  shirt  stir
skirt  third  birth

**SC**

scrap  scald  scale  scalp  scar  scarf  scone
score  scooter  scout  scrape  scrub

**TR**

trip  trap  trot  trim  trade  trail  train
tramp  transport  tray  treat  trench

**CR**

crab  crack  craft  crane  crash  cream  creep
cricket  crisp  crook  crop  cross

**FL**

flag  flake  flame  flap  flash  flat  fleet  fling
float  flour  flu  fly

**-GE**

cage  age  rage  wage  stage  page  hedge
edge  garage  bridge  hinge  lodge

## Group Five

### SK
skip  skirt  skate  skill  skid  skull  task  mask
ask  sketch  desk  flask

### PL
plum  plot  plan  plant  plank  plug  plump
place  plain  plastic  plate  play

### TW
twin  twig  twelve  twice  twist  twine  twinkle
twenty  between

### SL
slip  slot  slam  slug  slit  slap  slab  slate
slave  sleep  slice  slide

### PR
pram  prop  print  press  prank  pray  present
price  prick  prince  prize  prod

### FR
from  fringe  friend  frill  frame  free  freeze
fresh  frock  frog  frost  fruit

### SM
smile  smug  smoke  smack  small  smart  smash
smell  smudge  smut  smear  blacksmith

### -Y
happy  sunny  silly  funny  soapy  ('-y' sounding as
pretty                              'ee')
sky  my  fly  cry  dry  by  ('-y' sounding as 'i'—
                              usually monosyllabic
                              words)

## Group Six

### GL
glad  glance  glass  gleam  glide  glimpse
glitter  globe  gloom  glove  glow  glut

### WH
why  when  what  where  wheel  wheat  which
while  whine  whip  whisper  white

## UR
burn    turn    hurt    fur    curl    turnip    burst
churn    curtain    murder    Saturday    murmur

## DR
drip    drop    drum    drag    drain    drill    draw
dream    dress    drink    drive    drug

## SW
swim    swap    sweet    swill    sweep    swell    swift
swing    swot    swoop    swipe    switch

## SN
snip    snap    sniff    snug    snack    snake    snatch
sneeze    snob    snow    snug    snuff

## QU
queen    quite    quick    queer    quack    quantity
quarrel    quarter    quiet    quilt    quit    quiz

## -ED
kicked    dropped    killed    showed    filled    rowed
looked    locked    lasted    missed    robbed    mixed

# Group Seven

## OY
toy    boy    enjoy    royal    annoy    employ

## PH
telephone    graph    triumph    orphan    nephew
alphabet    telegraph    photograph    elephant
pheasant    phrase    physics

## AU
taut    autumn    caught    taught    August
Australia    author    autograph    automatic    cause
haunt    pause

## OI
coin    oil    toil    ointment    avoid    point    boil
join    joint    spoil    soil    foil

## EW
new    few    dew    crew    newt    screw    jewels
stew    chew    flew    knew    blew

**KN**

know    knot    knight    knee    kneel    knife    knit
knob    knock    knew    knowledge    knuckle

**WR**

wrap    wreck    wrestle    wriggle    wring    wrist
write    wrong    wrote    wren    wrench    wretch

**IGH**

tight    night    right    fright    might    bright    high
sigh    light    fight    flight    slight

*-ION and -OUS*

attention    tension    suspicion    distraction    division
action    jealous    tremendous    famous    precious
suspicious    delicious

## Sessions One-Five

The number of sessions this part of the programme will take is variable, but five sessions should be adequate if they are each of about thirty minutes.

We are going to make a reading book, which we shall call Phonic Reading Book 1A, using the words from Group One of the preceding lists; the programme will be repeated six times to cover the remaining six groups of words. Tailoring what you and your child write to include these words means that this part of the programme is going to seem more artificial and contrived than before. Thorough preparation on your part will make it less so. I make no apologies for the structure of a systematic approach; to the failed reader, who is always a *confused* reader, order and system come as a refreshing change.

You will need a plain drawing book, as before, and a red and a black ballpen or fibre-tip pen; the red pen will be used for those digraphs which are being learnt so that they stand out from the rest of the word (which will be written in black). Obviously, in the course of

making the book, you will use other digraphs apart from those you are studying specially. *Do not attempt to teach these.* At the same time, try to minimise the use of words containing complex phonic units other than the basic seven or eight.

On the inside front cover of the book copy the list of words which are going to be used. You start by explaining to the child that together you are going to make a reading book using the words that have these special combinations of letters which make their own sound. Emphasise that it is going to be a joint production, because you will need to have a good deal of control over what goes into the book. Explain that you are going to write about a number of topics that will enable you to use the special words on the inside front cover of the book. Tell your child that he can do the illustrations as you go along. The placing of the illustrations should be determined more by the need to provide a change and vary the pattern than by the requirements of the narrative. Tell him that the task is to learn the special sounds that are made by more than one letter, rather than learning any new words.

Each time one of the words is used, put a check mark against it in your list; this will give you a continuous guide to coverage. A frequency of between five and ten for each digraph is adequate, but as many different words as possible should be used—don't use the same word ten times!

Before you actually begin writing anything, go through the sounds and get your child to repeat them; do this until he can say them clearly—don't try to get him to memorise them at this stage. Spend some time discussing the sort of things you might write about, bearing in mind the words that have to be worked in. When you do start, remember to write the digraphs which are being learnt in red; in addition, break up *all* polysyllabic words into their separate syllables by drawing a red line down between the syllables.

A typical session might be writing a couple of pages, doing a couple of drawings, and then reading through. Any words of one syllable your child doesn't know you can say for him, but don't worry about trying to learn them. When you come to polysyllabic words, sound them out with him, demonstrating how you do your blending, a syllable at a time. However, when you come to a word containing a digraph in red, say, 'Now you sound this one out.' With these words help him only if necessary and spend enough time on each word to ensure that he sounds it out properly and makes a fair attempt at blending. Don't try to make it perfect; a reasonable approximation is all that is required. I must emphasise at this point that children do vary greatly in the facility with which they can do this. If it seems that your child needs to take it slowly, then set your pace accordingly. It really is of no consequence if it takes you six or seven sessions to complete your book.

Finally, phonics does not give entree to *all* words—some defy even the most elaborate phonic 'rules'. These are usually common words ('should' and 'said', for example) and many of them will have been learnt by sight in the first part of the programme. This technique remains the best way of dealing with them, but at the present stage such learning can be expected to occur incidentally.

| ee | //////// | ch |
|---|---|---|
| //////// | ay | //////// |

| sh | //////// | er |
|---|---|---|
| //////// | ck | th |

## Session Six

Phonic lotto: this is a good way to get the sounds and the letters firmly linked together before going on to further exercises in blending, discrimination, and so on. You can play this perfectly well with just yourself and the child under instruction. Make two cards with three or four digraphs on each (leave out the word ending) and small individual cards to call from. This makes rather a 'thin' game during the making of the first book, but as you progress on to the other books the cards should be accumulated and used all together, which vastly improves the game. During the first stages, four or five games of this will not be too much. When the same sounds are represented by more than one digraph, for example, 'ee' and 'ea', both count as far as the players are concerned—irrespective of what is on the caller's card.

L. I. H. E.

THE B____ ____Y

WOOLTON

'ND

## Session Seven

Get your child to read through the book out loud and, as far as possible, *without sounding out*; prompt him on any words where he hesitates and do this quickly so as to keep his reading fluent.

## Session Eight

Phonic flash cards: make a card for each digraph and make these large—about three inches square. Expose each card initially for five seconds, prompting if necessary. Speed up presentation progressively and finish the session when each one is recognised immediately.

## Session Nine

Phonic word building: this means making individual letter cards and cards for the digraphs/word endings and building words up from these. The size of the cards

is not very important, but it is better to have them too big than too small. You will need one card each for the digraphs/word endings and these should be in red; the individual letter cards should be written in black and you need a few for each letter of the alphabet.

Taking each of the digraph cards in turn say, 'You know what this says, let's see if we can make up one of the words in our book using these other cards' (indicating the individual letter cards). This is normally done very quickly. Then say, 'Can you think of any other words that have this in them?' (Point to the digraph card.) If your child can't think of one, you suggest a word and ask him to build it up, helping him if necessary. Do this with three or four words for each digraph.

Don't bother about making a list of the words or learning them—what you are teaching is a number of relationships and the way in which they operate.


## Sessions Ten and Eleven

Give your child the reading book you made and, providing him with a smaller book and a black pen, ask him to copy out its contents, without the illustrations and without writing the digraphs in red. Depending on how rapidly he writes and how much was written in the first place, this will take either one or two sessions. We will call this Phonic Reading Book 1B. Assuming that you let him get halfway through, you then ask him to read out loud what he has written; any words that cause hesitation should be sounded out after you have divided them up syllabically.

## Session Twelve

For each digraph/word ending, select two words which have not been used already. You are going to dictate these to your child who will attempt to sound them out and write them on a blackboard (or something similar). This is really quite a difficult task and will show you just how effective his discrimination of the phonic structure of words is. Take this slowly, supporting the sounding out in an unobtrusive way if necessary.

It will have taken you about three weeks to work through this first stage. Allow a week's break before starting on the next batch of digraphs, but during that week provide some reading books from the lists on the following pages. The books are divided into three groups: those in the first group are of a level suitable to be read after stages one and two of this section; those in the second group after books three, four and five; and the third group after books six and seven.

In tackling the remaining groups of digraphs, the pattern should be the same as outlined in this first stage. Do not attempt specific revision of those digraphs dealt with at earlier stages. The only exception to this rule is in phonic lotto, where new cards are added to the previous ones (or combined to make larger ones) in order to give the game greater variety.

# Recommended reading books (Section Three)

## GROUP ONE

| Series | Books | Author | Publisher |
|---|---|---|---|
| Keywords Reading Scheme (Ladybird) | 6a, 6b | W. Murray | Wills and Hepworth |
| Griffin Readers | 5, 6 | S. McCullagh | E. J. Arnold |
| Adventures in Reading | 5, 5a | G. Keir | Oxford University Press |
| Oxford Colour Reading Books | (4) A-F | C. Carver and C. H. Stowasser | Oxford University Press |
| Racing to Read | 9-12 | A. E. Tansley and R. H. Nicholls | E. J. Arnold |
| Dolphin Books | A1-A12 | Editor: Boswell Taylor | University of London Press Ltd. |

## GROUP TWO

| Series | Books | Author | Publisher |
|---|---|---|---|
| Keywords Reading Scheme (Ladybird) | 7a, 7b | W. Murray | Wills and Hepworth |

| Griffin Readers | 7, 8 | S. McCullagh | E. J. Arnold |
|---|---|---|---|
| Adventures in Reading | 6, 6a | G. Keir | Oxford University Press |
| More Adventures in Reading | 1, 2, 2a | G. Keir | Oxford University Press |
| Oxford Colour Reading Books | (5) A-F | C. Carver and C. H. Stowasser | Oxford University Press |
| Racing to Read | 13-16 | A. E. Tansley and R. H. Nicholls | E. J. Arnold |
| Dolphin Books | B1-B12 | Editor: Boswell Taylor | University of London Press Ltd. |

## GROUP THREE

| *Series* | *Books* | *Author* | *Publisher* |
|---|---|---|---|
| Keywords Reading Scheme (Ladybird) | 8a, 8b | W. Murray | Wills and Hepworth |
| Griffin Readers | 9, 10 | S. McCullagh | E. J. Arnold |

| | | | |
|---|---|---|---|
| More Adventures in Reading | 3, 3a | G. Keir | Oxford University Press |
| Oxford Colour Reading Books | (6) A-B | C. Carver and C. H. Stowasser | Oxford University Press |
| Dolphin Books | C1-C12 | Editor: Boswell Taylor | University of London Press Ltd. |

# Conclusion

If you have gone through the programme in this book in the manner and in the spirit that I have advocated, then your child should have achieved a broad mastery of all the major skills involved in reading. In other words, he will have arrived at the threshold of literacy, for real literacy *begins* at this point. The ability to recognise words and comprehend their meaning is a skill, or rather a compound of skills, and it is on this basis that an appreciation of the quality of written language will develop. And, of course, this is what literacy is really about. In writing this short book I have been keenly aware that at times the instruction programme seems rather mechanical and I can sympathise with those educationists who feel there must be a more elevated way of reaching the same goal. Unfortunately, learning to read just by motivation alone doesn't seem to work, attractive though the idea may be. Even a child who has worked successfully through this programme will need a great deal of further experience and consolidation before an easy fluency is achieved. The main requirements for continued progress are practice, a good deal of praise and encouragement, and a little direction and correction.

Writing is a great cementer of reading skills and this should be encouraged in every way possible, for example by making a project book, a diary, or a story book. Particular attention should be paid to the over-learning of common words that are spelt incorrectly.

Continued reading practice at an appropriate level is also important and I attach at the end of this section a list of books suitable for children who have achieved a moderate competence in reading. These books are, however, still 'readers' and they should soon be superseded by regular borrowings from the public library.

To achieve full literacy, your child must enjoy the experience of reading and writing. It would be fine if all children could learn to read as they learn to speak, absorbing it from their environment. But if direct instruction has its undesirable features, these are nothing compared to the demoralising effect of a failure to learn to read. And anyone who has seen the satisfaction of a child who has been helped to overcome reading failure will know that this is one of the few ways in which we can have a simple and direct effect on the happiness and general adjustment of children.

| Series | Books | Author | Publisher |
|---|---|---|---|
| Keywords Reading Scheme (Ladybird) | 9a, 9b, 10a, 10b | W. Murray | Wills and Hepworth |
| More Adventures in Reading | 4, 4a, 5, 5a, 6, 6a | G. Keir | Oxford University Press |
| Griffin Readers | 11, 12 | S. McCullagh | E. J. Arnold |
| Dolphin Books | D1-D12, E1-E6 | Editor: Boswell Taylor | University of London Press Ltd. |
| Challenge Books | 1-15 | A. E. Smith | Holmes McDougall |

Once fair to strong phonic skills have been established there are many series which can be found in most good bookshops and which should provide plenty of practice and a range of interest for the young reader. Among these the following can be recommended:

| | |
|---|---|
| *Young Puffins** | Penguin Books |
| *Brock Books* | Brockhampton Press |
| *Armada Lions** | Collins |
| *Knight Books** | Brockhampton Press |
| *Young World Books** | Nelson |
| *Grasshopper Books** | Abelard Schuman |
| *Real and Pretend Books* | Pitman |

The last series has some titles which are particularly suitable for boys.

* Indicates a paperback or part paperback series.

NOTRE DAME COLLEGE OF EDUCATION.
MOUNT PLEASANT. LIVERPOOL L3 5SP